Beautiful
North Carolina

"Learn about America in a beautiful way."

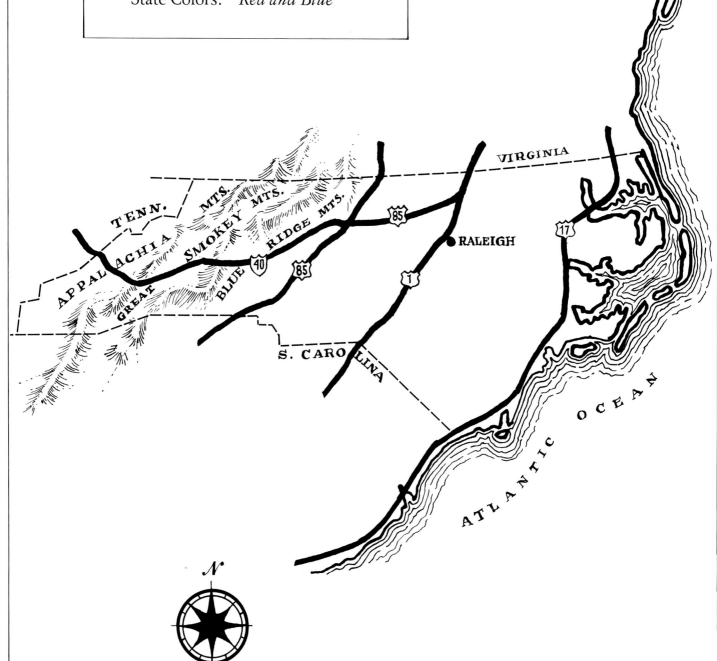

North Carolina

State Flower: *Dogwood*
State Nickname: *Tar Heel State*
State Bird: *Cardinal*
State Animal: *Gray Squirrel*
State Colors: *Red and Blue*

Beautiful
North Carolina

Concept and Design: Robert D. Shangle
Text: John Michael Fagan

First Printing May, 1980
Published by Beautiful America Publishing Company
P.O. Box 608, Beaverton, Oregon 97075
Robert D. Shangle, Publisher

Library of Congress Cataloging in Publication Data
Beautiful North Carolina
1. North Carolina—Description and travel—1951—Views. I. Title.
F255.F33   917.56'04'4   79-18081
ISBN 0-89802-075-1
ISBN 0-89802-074-3 (paperback)

Photo Credits

Contents

Introduction

Anyone who takes pleasure in spectacular mountains, lush farmlands, and hypnotic sunsets mirrored by the ocean is certain to have a romance with North Carolina.

One needs only to glance at a map to decide that the Old North State offers a love affair for all who visit its soil. The east side is washed by the Atlantic Ocean and the west side meets the highest mountain peaks east of the Mississippi River, the Great Smoky Mountains.

The Tar Heel State is separated into three natural divisions: the Coastal playgrounds, the rich and gently rolling farmlands and hills of the Piedmont, and the Western Highlands, a mountain haven and health resort.

''The goodliest land under the cope of heaven'' is how the first explorers described this land of varied spectacle. The rocky disposition of the Blue Ridge and Smoky Mountains, coupled with the dark loam, red clay of the Piedmont, and white sands of the coast beckon the visitor to set camp here.

Endless variety is one of North Carolina's greatest assets . . . rugged mountains and rustic log cabins, lush farmlands with colorful pockets of tobacco and peanut crops, and cotton fields swaying by the dictates of winds rolling off the mountains or in from the Atlantic.

A student of architecture can enjoy the natives' appreciation for the preservation of historical structures as well as their knack of gracefully melding new development with all parts of the remarkably beautiful countryside. Architecture swings from the hand-built log cabins of the Blue Ridge Mountains to the stately Georgian buildings of Duke University and colonial structures in Old Salem. This ''goodliest state'' does indeed appreciate its rich history, manifested in its architectural triumphs.

Historic sites and restorations dot the state, demonstrating the Tar Heels' appreciative attitude toward their forefathers' pioneer settlements. Historic Bethabara, located only minutes away from Winston-Salem, is the site of the first Moravian settlement in North Carolina. Founded in 1753, Bethabara became a trading center where fine craft wares could be bought. The 1788 Church and Gemeinhaus (meeting hall) has been restored and is one of the finest examples of Moravian architecture in America.

North Carolina's nickname is the Tar Heel State. Opinions on the origin differ according to whom you talk to. A commonly accepted version places the origin in the days of the War Between the States. In Colonial times, tar, pitch, and turpentine, all derived from the state's official tree, the pine, were the principal products. During one of the most grisly battles of the War Between the States, troops supporting the North Carolinans were greeted by a regiment coming up from the rear questioning: ''Any more tar down in the Old North State, boys?'' The answer was: ''No, not a bit, President Jeff Davis has bought it all up.'' ''Is that so? What's he going to do with it?'' ''He's going to put it on your heels to make you stick better in the next fight.'' When General Robert E. Lee heard of the incident, he said: ''God bless the Tar Heel boys.'' And so the name stuck.

A second opinion places the origin in the days of the Revolutionary War. Residents of Rocky Mount, a town in the northeast section of the Piedmont, assert the truth of the story. When citizens of this town learned that General Cornwallis was confiscating supplies of tar on his northward march from Wilmington to Virginia, they emptied their supply into the Tar River before his arrival. The tar remained soft on the river bed. Soldiers bathing in the stream were angry after finding the tar sticking to their feet. From then on, when a British soldier met a North Carolinian, he called the native a ''Tarheel.''

North Carolina's state motto, *Esse Quam Videri*—''To be, rather then to seem,'' is characteristic of its people. Although it is difficult to generalize about the people of the Tar Heel heritage, lack of pretense and an unwillingness to be impressed with sham seem to be fundamental traits.

Perhaps these characteristics stem partly from pioneer days. English, Scottish, German, and Moravian settlers lived by the work of their own hands. The plantation system never developed in the Piedmont on a large scale. And those settlers who pioneered the Highlands were forced by isolation to become self-sufficient and independent. Slavery, developed to a greater extent in some of their neighboring southern states, was virtually unknown to these pioneers.

It was the English who first successfully colonized the North Carolina and Virginia region after the Spanish and French attempts failed. In 1584, Sir Walter Raleigh sent an expedition to the New World to explore the coast and select a site for colonization. Roanoke Island, an island located between the mainland and the long chain of islands off the North Carolina coast, was chosen. Upon returning to their European homeland, expedition leaders Captain Amadas and Arthur Barlowe, reported that the soil was ''the most plentiful, sweete, fruitful and wholesome of all the world.'' They named the new land Virginia, honoring Queen Elizabeth I. Maybe, because the settlers were forced to navigate water on all sides to further explore the coast, Roanoke Island was the site of two false starts. The first permanent colony was established at Jamestown, Virginia in 1607. Gradually, explorers, hunters, traders, and settlers flowed into the New World colony, establishing themselves in the hinterland—the Albemarle section of North Carolina, a part of the southern Piedmont. By 1765, North Carolina was the fourth most populous English colony.

Anytime of the year and anywhere in the state, family entertainment opportunities abound. Dozens of boat shows, farm shows, theatre, and fiddling contests are held in the Old North State. A World Champion Old Time Fiddlers Convention is a special treat for those interested in North Carolina's true old time spirit and cultural flavor. Held yearly, the convention hosts the oldest, and best fiddlers from around the nation.

People find the climate of this state especially attractive. Natives are reminded about the pleasantries of their home climate only when out-of-state visitors arrive and praise its healing virtues. A warm temperate zone, modified by the great variety of topography, is what partly endears so many to the Tar Heel State. Warm summer breezes greet the sun worshiper along the coast, while in the mountains, a chill invigorates hikers ready for adventure in boundless acres of forest lands. Periods of extreme heat and cold are infrequent in any part of the state.

This state offers so much stunning scenery, warm hospitality, and abundant family entertainment, that it is sure to establish, for the visitor in any season, a life-long romance.

The Piedmont And The Coastal Plains

Distinctive geographical features and a wide variety of industries highlight the large swath of land situated between the North Carolina coast and the western highlands.

Known as the Coastal Plains and the Piedmont, these lowlands offer excellent recreational opportunities, numerous all-year historical attractions, and a look at the business and industrial sectors of the North Carolina state.

The character and destiny of this interior section has been enriched by the cornerstones of North Carolina's famed ''Research Triangle,'' Duke University and the two state institutions, University of North Carolina and North Carolina State.

North Carolina State University, the agricultural and technical branch of the state college system, is two miles west of the Capitol, Raleigh. North Carolina State's noted School of Design casts its influence on the University's newer buildings and the striking J.S. Dorton Arena on the State Fairgrounds a few miles south on Hillsborough Street. This parabolic pavilion is used for livestock judging, rodeos, and exhibits during Fair Week in early October. One of the largest fairs on the eastern seaboard, the fair incorporates exhibits ranging from Indian arts and crafts to modern day technology.

Contrast is everywhere. The sheen of newness reflected by shopping centers and night clubs of the city is just further than a stone's throw from hills rolling with cotton and tobacco—the country life.

The North-Central quarter of the Piedmont is alive with the 'new of North Carolina.' Fine restaurants, department stores, and pleasant residential suburbs—signs of the good life—are highlights of cities like Winston-Salem, Raleigh, Greensboro, Durham, and High Point.

A good introduction to the Piedmont is Raleigh, the Capitol. It is located on US 1 and on two main east-west highways, US 70 and US 64. Visitors can tour the historic Capitol (1840) and Legislative Building, the Museum of History, and the Art Museum.

The governmental buildings are located in the downtown areas of Raleigh. Large and graceful, the Capitol building exemplifies fine Grecian Doric architecture. During the upheaval of the days of reconstruction after the Revolutionary War, the west wing was used as a barroom for "carpetbaggers" and "scalawag" legislators. Nicks on the floor still show where the whiskey barrels had been rolled in and out of the legislative chambers. The nearby legislative building has been called the most beautiful of its kind in the nation. Of contemporary design, it is located less than a block from the Capitol.

The visitor interested in touring all of the public attractions won't be disappointed. The art fancier will glow with delight over the Art Museum's multi-million dollar collection of masterworks. It displays the work of past masters and contemporary painters. The museum's enviable collection is ranked among the top 17 in the nation. Also featuring the first art gallery for the blind, it was the nation's first art museum whose collections were funded with state monies.

One mile from Capitol Square is President Andrew Johnson's small cabin home. Johnson's living quarters served as a guest house for members of the General Assembly. It was originally located about a block from the Capitol Building. The 17th president was the first to experience an unglorious impeachment trial; however, he was acquitted by a single vote following a heated and bitter Senate trial which exposed charges of the leader's compassion toward the South during the Reconstruction Period.

Another President, more favored in history and a native of North Carolina, is Andrew Jackson. Known as "Old Hickory," Jackson was born in Union County near the South Carolina state line. Due to a boundary dispute, South Carolina also claims to be his home. Jackson studied law in Salisbury and was licensed and practiced law in Greensboro.

When a visitor is ready for a change of scenery from the city, he can discover the beauty of North Carolina's greatest gift—the beauty of the land, including all its greenery. Seventy miles south of Raleigh in the southern Piedmont, white sand and longleaf pines distinguish an area known as the Sandhills. Nestled away from the urban Piedmont cities are the year-round resort towns of Pinehurst and Southern Pines. Here is a golfers' paradise. The only private golf club in the world boasting *five* 18-hole courses, the Pinehurst Country Club attracts the year-round golf enthusiast. The town of Pinehurst is a home for leisurely lifestyle, with beautiful estates and comfortable hotels and inns offering rest and comfort to all visitors. In the Southern

Pines-Pinehurst area are additional golf courses worthy of all challengers. Due to the southern Piedmont's moderate climate, golf can usually be enjoyed year-round in the Sandhills area.

U.S. Presidents seem to keep returning to North Carolina. Gerald Ford officiated at the opening of the World Golf Hall of Fame at Pinehurst in 1974. Total tournament purses exceeded $1 million, underlining the state's reputation as "Golf State U.S.A."

But there's no reason for non-golfers to stay away from the Sandhills. For vacationers who look beyond the golf greens, the Sandhills offers racing of both the horse and motor variety. Horses—the racing and showing thereof—are a popular leisure-time activity in this region, and traditional foxhunts—with hounds, costumes, and trumpets—are regular events.

Not far from the Sandhills is Rockingham, home of the North Carolina Motor Speedway. The Carolina 500 and the American 500 are staged here every year, making Rockingham a major point in American stock-car racing. Rumor has it that stock-car racing in the south is merely a carry-over from another southern tradition: bootlegging. The first "stock car races" were reputedly held on southern backroads. Participants cars were hot-rodded for speed and handling, and especially equipped with tanks for carrying distilled products—and the Internal Revenue agents whose job it was to catch them. Of course, that's the kind of rumor that nobody will exactly verify—and it's nothing but an interesting sidelight to the multi-million dollar sport which is stock-car racing today.

Not to be overlooked while strolling in the neighborhood of Pinehurst are the beautifully manicured Clarendon Gardens. The garden overflows with 20 acres of winter plants. The American Holly Society has recognized Clarendon as one of the nation's top holly collections. Frequent tours are conducted throughout the area.

To the east is the busier life with the cultural influences offered to those who are fascinated by all that human industry is capable of producing. Charlotte is a busy center of trade, manufacturing, transportation, and communication. Named for Queen Charlotte of Mecklenburg, wife of George III, the "Queen City" is the state's largest convention host, and is easily accessible in the southeastern portion of the Piedmont. Major events include the Festival in the Park, featuring North State creative works at their best: arts and crafts reflective of North Carolina's culture and heritage. Beautiful flower shows coupled with frequent tours of Charlotte's most exquisite homes help endear this hospitable city to all visitors.

The proud citizens of Charlotte will likely tell you how Charlotte came to be known as the "Hornet's Nest." When General Cornwallis and his British troops entered Charlotte in 1780, they met such ferocious resistance during their occupation of the town that, exasperated, they compared the confrontation to meeting up with a hornet's nest. The townspeople proudly adopted the nickname for their city; and it has lasted a long time.

Also worth a stroll in this city of diversified interests is the Mint Museum of Art. Back in the days when the state was the nation's largest gold producer, the building served as a branch of the U.S. Mint—from 1837 to 1913. The building now houses a permanent collection of paintings, porcelain, and sculpture.

The beauty of North Carolina is manifested when the newcomer recognizes the state's great versatility. After enjoying all of the cultural assets of the city, the unhurried traveler can head north of Charlotte to enjoy one of North Carolina's natural gifts—water. Lake Norman, formed by Cowan's Ford Dam, is a few miles from Charlotte on the Catawba River. Covering more than 30,000 acres, this is the largest lake in the Tar Heel State. Duke Power State Park and many marinas and boat launching sites provide access to the recreation area.

With water sports on his mind, the visitor might also meander to Morrow Mountain State Park. Swimming, boating, fishing, camping, and hiking—a whole world for the outdoorsman—is available in this spacious and breathtaking mountain resort located only 42 miles northeast of Charlotte. A scenic drive to the top of Morrow Mountain can open an appreciative eye to more natural wonders of this state. Morrow Mountain is one of a series of peaks of the Uwharrie Range. The incomparable Uwharries, partly protected for future generations by national forest status, stretch across parts of four counties.

Located near the heart of North Carolina's great industrial centers is Old Salem. A meticulously restored community reminiscent of a Moravian congregation town some 200 years ago, Old Salem residents are proud to tell you the ancient story of their home. Founded by people of the former Czech-Slovak Republic, Moravia, Old Salem was settled in 1766. The old town still reflects the character and color of its founding days. Several buildings, including the Home Moravian Church (1800) and several units on the Salem College campus, have been in continuous use since the late 1700s and early 1800s. Tours, and history lessons generously filled with anecdotes about ''my granddaddy's days'' are held through the year in the town, which covers about six blocks. History buffs will be fascinated with the Salem Tavern, built in 1783. Taken back in time, the guest will visit the oldest tobacco shop still standing in the U.S., the Hiksch Tobacco Shop of 1773. Also open to the public are the homes of the village silversmith and clockmaker.

On the road again, the visitor can step from the heart of American history into the mainstays of the state's economy, industrial centers of Winston-Salem and Durham. Winston-Salem is a combination of two communities: Salem with the traditions of its Moravian founders, and industrial Winston. Located here is R.J. Reynolds Tobacco Company, one of the world's largest tobacco manufacturing centers. In addition, the Joseph Schlitz Brewing Company produces more than four million barrels of beer annually. Both companies offer tours of their spacious facilities.

A gift to the public by Mr. and Mrs. William Reynolds, of Reynolds Tobacco fame, is Tanglewood Park. Situated eight miles west of Winston-Salem at Clemmons, the 1,117-acre estate is, without contest, one of the most beautiful and complete recreation resorts in the country. Located on the Yadkin River, golf courses, tennis courts, camping and swimming facilities, horseback riding trails and summer theater are all available to the appreciative visitor. This is a place where a person can put aside all concept of time, forget worries and enjoy the life of his dreams. In addition, in the center of the park is the gracious manor house where visitors may dine. Tanglewood was the site of the 1974 Professional Golf Association Championship Tournament.

Returning to interests in commerce and industry, Durham is located in the northwestern sector of the Piedmont. Durham is a ranking industrial center, leading tobacco producer and home of Duke University. History of the city is characteristic of an American success story. It has been said that James B. Duke did with tobacco what Rockefeller did with oil and Carnegie with steel. He began by grinding tobacco which he packaged and sold. By 1874, Duke and his three sons were established as manufacturers of smoking tobacco. Within a few years, they were producing cigarettes for domestic sale and export. The growth of the huge American Tobacco empire and related enterprises started here in Durham.

Duke University, which bears the tobacco king's name and is the principal beneficiary of the Duke Endowment, is located only five minutes from the Durham business district. Buildings on the east campus are of Georgian architecture while the west campus is built in Gothic style, reminiscent of Oxford and Cambridge, England. Dominating all of the campus is Duke Chapel, rising 210 feet above the ground.

Historic Hillsborough is located just east of Durham. It was here that the uprising of the Regulators, some 2,000 Alamance farmers, was culminated in defeat at the Battle of Alamance on May 16, 1771. Many historians agree that this battle was the first major conflict of the American Revolution. The battlefield, where six of the offenders were captured and hanged, is now restored as a State Historic Site. The courthouse, completed in 1845, contains an unbroken sequence of wills and deeds from 1756 to the present. In the cupola is the famous clock, which tradition holds was donated to the town by George III, Earl of Hillsboro. Many of the town's fine old homes have been restored to their original grandeur.

Not to be ignored in travelers' plans are the broad and peaceful coastal plains to the east. Although agriculture is not limited to any particular section of the state, the central and southeastern portions contain some of the richest farmland in eastern America. Diversified farming has demonstrated remarkable success with products including flowers, strawberries, cotton, corn, tobacco, soybeans, and Irish potatoes. Patches of color tranquilize the visitor who gazes upon the vast acreage in these rolling hills which eventually end at the Atlantic ocean.

The Coast

Amountain man or resident of the midlands will direct you to ''down yonder'' when you ask for the coast. The North Carolina coastline is a museum of pirate history and a playground of sun and sea. It is a place rich in marine folklore, where one can confirm tall tales by waiting for a low tide to uncover waterlogged skeletons of more than 2,000 North Carolina vessels.

''Down Yonder,'' is roughly one-third of the state and covers a broad sweep of sandy beaches and accessible islands—lots of open space for the adventurous.

The coast is a flavorful mix of barbecue, steamed clams, brunswick stew, tobacco, peanuts, and livestock. It is a land of the pine and white oak, the flowering crepe myrtle, the chinaberry and the Yaupon trees. In short, this land is a paradise endowed with a fascinating past and an incomparably beautiful present. The visitor, who sheds his wristwatch and dives into the wide variety of coastal playgrounds, can enjoy the water and sun at day, while at night he can be awed by the whispered stories of pirate treasure and of early pioneer triumphs.

A most thorough method for exploring North Carolina's waterways is to begin on Highway 158 near the Virginia border. Ninety miles from the start of this modern all-weather highway is the first of North Carolina's chain of seaside resorts, historical Kitty Hawk. It was here in 1900 that Orville and Wilbur Wright began glider experiments leading to the first powered flight on December 17, 1903. The isolation of this site and suitable weather and wind conditions brought the Wright brothers to this spot. For 12 seconds, man's first heavier-than-air craft powered itself 120 feet above ground. On the fourth flight it flew 852 feet in 59 seconds.

Kitty Hawk has a rich story, too, about pirates and their notorious plundering of trade ships. It is believed that the beautiful Theodosia Burr, daughter of Aaron Burr, was made to walk the plank somewhere in the vicinity. On December 30, 1812, she sailed from Georgetown, South Carolina on the *Patriot*, a small pilot boat, to visit her father in New York, and was never seen again. The boat was believed to have been wrecked off Cape Hatteras, further south, during a storm.

In 1869, a physician named W.G. Pool responded to a call by a poor and ailing woman, who gave him a portrait in place of a fee, and revealed to him its story. The story linked the picture to Theodosia's actual tragedy. According to the woman, in 1812, a small pilot boat, with sails set and rudder lashed, drifted ashore at Kitty Hawk. There were no signs of bloodshed or violence on the deserted ship; an untouched meal was on the table, and silk dresses hung within the cabin. On the wall was the portrait of a young and beautiful woman, painted in oil on polished mahogany and set in a gilded frame. After the boat was stripped, the portrait was returned to the woman's sweetheart who gave it to her. It was believed that the pirates had forced all on board to walk the plank, only to be frightened away before they could plunder the ship.

Dr. Pool was impressed by the remsemblance of his newfound portrait to pictures of Aaron Burr. Photographs of the portrait were sent to members of the Burr family, who identified the likeness of Theodosia. Legendary confessions later confirmed the tale. Years later, two criminals admitted they were members of the pirate crew that boarded the *Patriot* and forced its passengers to walk the plank. A dying beggar in a Michigan almshouse confessed he was one of the pirates, and that he had been haunted by the face of the beautiful woman who pleaded for her life, that she might go to her father in New York.

More legends and pirate stories accompany the visitor who continues traveling south along North Carolina's sandy beaches.

Approximately 30 miles from Kitty Hawk, the Nags Head resort area serves up adventure and unparalleled coastal beauty. In addition to untold miles of public beaches and popular resorts, Nags Head is the site of Jockey's Ridge, the nation's highest sand dune. Sand skiiers and hang-gliders find the 138-foot high dunes amenable to their idea of adventure in the coast sunshine. In addition, this is a photographer's dream, as the dunes constantly change landscape and shadows. Nags Head is said to earn its name from those unscrupulous land pirates who tied lanterns on the necks of ponies and marched them along the high dunes on the island. The swinging lights simulated lights of boats, tricking captains into running their ships aground on shoals where their cargo could be stolen.

Only a few miles away, near the town of Manteo on Roanoke Island, was the landing site of the first English colonists who appeared in 1585. Fort Raleigh—a restored English fortress—marks this area as one of America's great mysteries—the Lost Colony. Within the Fort Raleigh National Historic Site is Waterside Theater where the outdoor drama, ''The Lost Colony,'' presents the mysterious story of the disappearance of these first settlers. Adjacent to Fort Raleigh is the Elizabethan Garden, a ten-acre memorial to the colonists who vanished from their fortress.

Blue Valley, Nantahala National Forest

18

Cape Hatteras Lighthouse
(Following pages) Greenfield Gardens, Wilmington

North Carolina sunset
(Following pages) Arlie Gardens, Wilmington

Oconaluftee River, Great Smoky Mountain National Park

Pilots Knob (elevation 2,440 feet)

National Military Park
(Following page) Fishing trawler at Ocracoke

Farmland near Sparta

Rhododendron

Somerset Place Historic Site

Crabtree Falls

Salvo Beach, Cape Hatteras National Seashore

Looking Glass Falls

Cypress Trees, Somerset Place Historic Site

Sand dunes near Cape Hatteras National Seashore

Sunset, Pamlica Sound, Cape Hatteras National Seashore

Wildflowers along Blue Ridge Parkway
(Following pages) Scroll Garden, Orton Plantation Gardens, Wilmington

Shipwreck of the Altoona, Hatteras Island

Ledge Creek, Great Smoky National Park

Silver Lake on Ocracoke Island

Blue Ridge Parkway

48

Tryon Paine Gardens

Mile High Overlook, Great Smoky Mountains

Tanglewood Lake

Ocracoke Island

Airlie Gardens, Wilmington
(Following pages) Greenfield Gardens, Wilmington

Cascades of Falls Creek, E.B. Jeffress Park

55

Wild Rhododendron

58

Lush mountain foliage

Bodie Island Lighthouse, Cape Hatteras National Seashore

Soco Gap, Blue Ridge Parkway

63

Today, Roanoke Island separates the lake-filled mainland from the offshore islands. It serves as the window to the National Seashore Recreation Area, Cape Hatteras, and Cape Lookout Seashore—all long, snake-like islands lying just off the spacious sands of the Atlantic seaboard.

Virtually all corners of Hatteras Island are easily accessible from Highway 12, which extends like a concrete ribbon the entire length of the island. Free state ferries link the island—and the highway—with the mainland. The nation's first such recreational area, Cape Hatteras National Seashore, comprises 45 miles of undeveloped beaches and includes eight small fishing villages—some with lighthouses. Commercial enterprise is prohibited on this stretch, leaving the natural habitat open for ambitious hikers, fishermen, and campers. These islands provide some of the best surf fishing in the nation. Billfishing is the best here, say the locals.

Accessible by only sea and air is remote Ocracoke Island, just south of Cape Hatteras. Blackbeard is remembered here. Teacher's Hole, a slough near Ocracoke Inlet, bears the infamous pirate's real name, Edward Teach. A free state-operated ferry links Hatteras and Ocracoke Islands, and a toll ferry operates between the island and Cedar Island, across the wide Pamlico Sound to Morehead City.

Hundreds of seaport towns acquaint the sightseer with the characteristic Tar Heel charm and comfort. Morehead City and Beaufort, two neighboring fishing ports located on the mainland off the southernmost tip of Cape Lookout National Seashore, docks recreational boats as well as cargo ships. Dolphin, marlin, mackerel and other gamefish attract many experienced and neophyte fishermen, as well. Inland from Morehead is the second oldest town in North Carolina, New Bern. The city marks the joining of the Neuse and Trent Rivers, 35 miles inland from the sea. Tryon Palace and gardens, described as the ''most beautiful building in Colonial America,'' is one of dozens of historical attractions in New Bern. The stately mansion was erected in 1770. The first capitol of North Carolina, New Bern barely escaped obscurity in 1711 when the population was almost wiped out by rampaging Tuscarora Indians.

Bath is another inland city situated on the Pamlico River. Nearby this historic city is the Pungo River and several beaches. Settled in 1696, Bath is the oldest town in the state. St. Thomas Episcopal Church, the state's oldest church building, is home for Sheffield silver candelabra from the period of English King George III. The church bell given by Queen Anne was firecast in England in 1732.

Wilmington is another history-enriched port located inland from the Cape Fear River along the far south coast. Rich in old homes, the city is a builder's dream. Sunken gardens entice many bees as well as visitors in pursuit of nature's colorful artistry. Here is the native home of the notorious Venus Fly Trap, a beautiful flowering plant that entraps insects.

Wildlife and incomparable plantlife are abundant all along the eastern seaboard. West of Elizabeth City, near Pasquotank River, is Ferry Swamp. The fragrant swamp woodlands of pine and cedar are alive with dogwood, honeysuckle, wild rose, and Carolina yellow jessamine. Cattails rise above the wind-blown reeds and smilax intertwines itself around the taller trees. Pecan groves line the highway on this beautiful stretch of coastline.

Migratory waterfowl in the form of white swans and many species of wild ducks and geese flock to several hiding places along the coast. Sportsmen travel from afar to Currituck to make use of several clubhouses and lodges that dot the islands and shore. Guides and boats are available for hunting and fishing trips in Manteo on Roanoke Island where wildlife abound.

For lovers of the water, the sun . . . for those who hunt and fish . . . and for those who can appreciate the bounty of seemingly unending and unexplored beaches, the North Carolina coastline is unmatched.

North Carolina Mountains

Some folks claim the spirit of Daniel Boone still walks the trails and byways of the North Carolina mountains. It's not too hard to believe; reminders of the past are all around, and the 20th century has laid a fairly light hand on these forested reaches. Perhaps it is the isolation, or the morning mists, or the simple serenity of the landscape that keeps the pioneer heritage so fresh. This land was cleared by pioneers who worked with the indomitable spirit of the new frontier, and that attitude carries over to the present generation, with today's "pioneers" stressing preservation. These folks have the pride and self-sufficiency that seems to be typical of mountain people—old Daniel Boone could be just around the corner.

Christian Reid, a North Carolina author, named this mountainous eastern section of the state "The Land of the Sky." This is a place where people can feel one with the sky—after all, this stretch of the Appalachians are some of the tallest east of the Mississippi, and are the oldest mountain range in the world. Log cabins and mountain streams, and the unending folklore of pioneering ancestors, make this a land of adventure . . . and the land of the sky.

The highest mountains in eastern America have wooed all manner of people in search of a quiet place of inspiring beauty. Carl Sandburg, poet and Lincoln biographer, chose his retirement home in these hills, where two centuries before, Daniel Boone carved trails in the isolated hills and valleys of the Great Smoky and Blue Ridge Mountains. It is no wonder that so many men of pioneering spirit have come and settled in this land where isolation breeds challenge. Survival skills teach the young and the old, the pioneer and the contemporary hiker, that the mountains of North Carolina are ones to be held in reverence and respect.

Western North Carolina has been apportioned a healthy chunk of the great Appalachian system which starts in New Hampshire and extends south into northern Alabama. On the east, these mountains are known as the Blue Ridge. A blue haze which seems perpetually to hang over this rugged country explains its given name. Further east are the Great Smoky Mountains, marking the state division between North Carolina and Tennessee. It is here that the Appalachians reach their highest and achieve their most massive size. Nearly 50 peaks soar over 6,000 feet in elevation, while nearly 175 peaks achieve the 5,000-foot mark. Mt. Mitchell dwarfs all other peaks east of the Mississippi River, measuring 6,684 feet.

Several national parks, dotted throughout the Blue Ridge and Great Smoky Mountains, make this extremely rugged country accessible for the traveler interested in fishing, hunting, hiking, and rockhounding. The Great Smoky Mountains National Park is said to be the nation's most visited national park. Containing almost 800 square miles of the wildest and most isolated highlands in the eastern United States, the park is a portion of the gigantic forest that once extended from the Atlantic coast to the midwest prairies. The park is shared almost equally by neighboring Tennessee. Although there are several entrances to mountain sites for camping, hiking, and fishing, Cherokee is the principal way into the park.

Located on US Highway 19, Cherokee introduces the adventuresome visitor to a part of North Carolina's rich Indian culture, as well as to its towering Smokies. The village of Cherokee is the hub of the largest organized Indian reservation east of Wisconsin. The North Carolina Cherokees still compete in archery and blowgun contests, play the traditional game of Indian stick ball, and participate in other games and dances that were begun long before the white man arrived. Part of the reservation lands were purchased and given to the Cherokees by William Thomas, the Government Indian Agent, himself part Indian. Later, the US government established the Qualls Boundary, official reservation of the Cherokee Nation. The reservation comprises about 50,000 acres in the heart of the Smokies. Each summer the sad story of the ''Trail of Tears''—when the Cherokee was torn from his native land and moved westward to Oklahoma during the severe and cruel winter—is told in Kermit Hunter's outdoor drama, ''Unto These Hills.'' The drama plays nightly, except Sunday, during the summer months.

An Indian museum boasts the largest collection of artifacts in the Cherokee Nation. Spear points and pottery, some 10,000 years old, attract the history buff to the reservation nestled in the mountains.

Clingman's Dome, located a few miles from the Cherokee Reservation on the Tennessee-North Carolina border, is a peak the lucky sightseer can gaze on forever. The third tallest peak in eastern America, Clingman's Dome sits atop a mountain 6,643 feet above sea level. Five states are visible: Tennessee, Virginia, South Carolina, Georgia, and the Tar Heel state.

National forests and rugged mountains appear to be unending here. Nantahala and Pisgah, two of North Carolina's four national forests, are located in these lush mountains. Nantahala, taking its name from the Cherokee Indian word meaning "land of the noonday sun," contains approximately 449,000 acres and was once a part of the Indian hunting grounds. Pisgah National Forest includes nearly 500,000 acres of lush forests. Both forests are ideal for family picnicking, camping, boating, hunting, fishing and whiling away the idle hours in the incomparable mountain air. Whitewater canoeing is a highlight for excitement in the swift streams leading to several lakes in the Nantahala Forest. Lake Hiwassee, Nantahala Lake, Lake Santeenah, and Fontana Lake are fed by fast-moving mountain streams ideal for the canoeist.

The Blue Ridge Parkway is a meandering ribbon of road which opens the traveler to the heart of forest beauty in the Blue Ridge Mountains. The Parkway, avoiding busy interstate freeways, begins at the northern border with Virginia and extends to the Cherokee Indian Qualla Boundary. Winding from the north, the Parkway encounters hundreds of parks, waterfalls, mountain peaks and gardens, all nestled in the vastness of the southern Appalachian Mountains.

Beckoning the sightseer who travels along the spacious Parkway is Linville Falls and Caverns, of Linville Gorge. The Falls takes its name from the spectacular falls and steep, wooded gorge of the Linville River. Incredible stalactites and stalagmites woo travelers off the road to Linville Caverns. Described as the most rugged wilderness in eastern America, Linville Gorge Wilderness Area has been set aside for future generations, so it will stay that way.

Just south on the Parkway is Little Switzerland, a comfortable mountain resort attracting artists, writers, and passersby. Much of the 1,200-acre summer colony is still wooded. Rustic inns and cottages invite the visitor with a preference for privacy. From a knoll directly behind the inn, spectacular Mount Mitchell is visible on a clear day. Continuing south, the visitor will be delighted by the Craggy Rhododendron Gardens. During blossoming season in June, this largest-known stand of purple rhododendron extends more than one mile in some places. The breathtaking blanket of rich rose and purple offers a restful sight for people who come from miles around to view the springtime splendor.

A short drive away is Zeb Vance's birthplace, a simple homestead. As Governor of North Carolina during the Civil War, Vance's opinion of that conflict was a "rich man's war and a poor man's fight." He reluctantly committed Tar Heel troops to the Confederate cause and then only after being assured that the North Carolina boys would be looked after properly and "would not have to serve under Virginia officers.'' Vance's birthplace, located north of Asheville, and accessible from the Parkway or via US 19-23 from Weaverville, has been restored and is now a State Historic Site.

Not far off the eastern Parkway route is one of several beautiful waterfalls, Looking Glass Falls. Tumbling from Looking Glass Rock, the falls are bathed in color during springtime. Both the falls and the mountain are named for the shimmering ice that accumulates on the mountainside during the winter months.

The highest mountaintop in the eastern U.S. is Mount Mitchell. It is said that you can look down on every earthly thing in the United States east of the Mississippi River from here. The summit is accessible via a toll-free highway through Mount Mitchell State Park.

Grandfather Mountain, located further north near Linville, is a place so revered by mountain natives that children hereabouts tell of having three grandfathers. In 1794, French botanist Andre Michaux climbed the mountain and sang the ''Marseillaise,'' believing he had discovered the highest point in North America.

In all, the Parkway offers every type of mountain scenery. There are hundreds of lookouts overlooking the Piedmont, verdant forests and clusters of village rooftops spotting the rolling farmlands. All of western North Carolina's mountainous region is a veritable showcase of vegetation, minerals, and fauna. Botanists have identified over 145 varieties of trees and more than 1,000 other plants here.

When planning a visit in the spring or autumn to witness the color parade of foliage, it is wise to consider two rules of thumb. Color begins in the high elevations and moves down the slopes; the earlier your trip, the higher the places you should plan your visit. Second, most color is best balanced between October 10 and 25. In most areas below 3,000 feet, the explosion of color continues until November.

Most sections of the highlands refresh the visitors' interest in the history of the region. Hewn-log dwellings are reminders of the homesteaders in this isolated frontier. Cluttered country stores dot the highlands with more reminders of the settlers' lifestyles. It is no wonder that the Tar Heel mountain men share an intense pride in their home. Burning independence and the unforgotten skills of the frontier have kept the spirit of Daniel Boone alive in this corner of North Carolina.

Enlarged Prints

Most of the photography in this book is available as photographic
enlargements. Send self-addressed, stamped envelope for information.
For a complete product catalog, send $1.00.
Beautiful America Publishing Company
P.O. Box 608
Beaverton, Oregon 97075

Beautiful America Publishing Company

The nation's foremost publisher of quality color photography

Current Books

Alaska, Arizona, British Columbia, California, California Vol. II, California Coast, California Desert, California Missions, Colorado, Florida, Georgia, Hawaii, Idaho, Las Vegas, Los Angeles, Michigan, Michigan Vol. II, Minnesota, Montana, Montana Vol. II, Mt. Hood (Oregon), New York, New Mexico, Northern California, Northern California Vol. II, North Carolina, North Idaho, Ohio, Oklahoma, Oregon, Oregon Vol. II, Oregon Coast, Oregon Country, Pennsylvania, Pittsburgh, San Diego, San Francisco, San Juan Islands, Seattle, Texas, Utah, Vancouver U.S.A., Virginia, Washington, Washington Vol. II, Washington D.C., Wisconsin, Wyoming, Yosemite National Park

Forthcoming Books

Beauty of Oregon, Beauty of Washington, Boston, California Mountains, Chicago, Dallas, Denver, Illinois, Indiana, Kentucky, Maryland, Massachusetts, Mississippi, Missouri, Nevada, New Jersey, New York City, Pacific Coast, Rocky Mountains, South Carolina, Tennessee, Vermont

Large Format, Hardbound Books

Beautiful America, Beauty of California, Glory of Nature's Form, Lewis & Clark Country, Western Impressions